WHEN WOMEN GATHER

WHEN WOMEN GATHER

Planning Guide for Conferences, Seminars, Workshops or Retreats

Naomi E. Peete
Theresa M. Taylor

Writers Club Press
New York Lincoln Shanghai

When Women Gather

Planning Guide for Conferences, Seminars, Workshops or Retreats

Writers Club Press
an imprint of iUniverse, Inc.

For information address:
iUniverse, Inc.
2021 Pine Lake Road, Suite 100
Lincoln, NE 68512
www.iuniverse.com

ISBN: 0-595-26792-0

Printed in the United States of America

To the Women of Mount Zion Baptist Church

who

follow after God's own heart.

To our beautiful and inspiring mothers:

Mrs. Ruth Edna Peete
Mrs. Merry Florence Cole

CONTENTS

▼

INTRODUCTION

Anything you say to a wise person will make them wiser. Whatever you say to a righteous person will add to their knowledge.

—Proverbs 9:9

INTRODUCTION

Anything you say to a wise man will make him wiser. Whatever you say to a righteous man will add to his knowledge.

—*Proverbs 9:9*

If you've chosen this book, it's because you want to do your very best to provide a successful gathering. You will have aspects that are unique to your particular group but you also want to learn from those who have done it before. This manual is a guide. You are encouraged to use these steps in creating a gathering, and you need to do them with a method or plan. Whether it's a large conference that will last a few days or a series of workshops, you need to have some kind of order. It is important for you to be thinking about all of the creative steps throughout the entire planning process. If you try to think about all of the aspects of putting together a gathering at one time, you would likely need a lot of time and energy to devote to it. However, if you try to execute each part of your plan mutually exclusive from the rest, you won't wind up with a very well-organized conference.

You need to be at least three and a half months away from your prospective gathering date. Four months is much better, meeting with your committee once per week. Some weeks might require more than one meeting and working on tasks away from the meetings as well.

Keep in mind that your committee may not be able to meet during summer or major holidays in December.

Each person on your committee needs to understand the effort it will take to plan a successful gathering, and everyone must be willing to follow it through to the end.

NOTES

VISION

Let all the nations be gathered together, and let the people be assembled: who among them can declare this, and show us former things? Let them bring forth their weaknesses, that they may be justified; or let them hear, and say, it is truth.

—Isaiah 43:9

VISION

Let all the nations be gathered together, and let the people be assembled: who among them can declare this, and show us former things? Let them bring forth their witnesses, that they may be justified: or let them hear, and say, it is truth.

—Isaiah 43:9

Planning a Woman's Gathering can be both exciting and overwhelming. You might feel you are going in five different directions at one time. This could leave you feeling unsure about the best way to pull together a seminar, conference or gathering.

The Vision for this guide is to help women who want to help others move forward and reach for higher expectations. Some might claim to undertake a conference or woman's gathering is a huge leap of faith over the Grand Canyon. That may be, but you do not need to jump blindly. This guide will hopefully be a beneficial tool for you to use. It is based on other women's experiences, victories and challenges in planning similar events. We have been where you are. Use this guide as a foundation for your creativity, a springboard for designing gatherings that will meet the specific needs of women in your community and a practical as well as economical method for women to share their faith. Remember your "I Cans" will outweigh your "I Can'ts" when you trust in your heart that you will be making a positive difference in someone's life.

VISION NOTES

PURPOSE

Look straight ahead with honest confidence, don't hang your head in shame. Plan carefully what you do, and whatever you do will turn out right.

—Proverbs 4:25-26

PURPOSE

The purpose of this manual is to enable you to benefit from the lessons experienced by others without having to go through all the difficulties. Also, it can be used as a foundation for creativity gatherings to meet specific needs.

For first-time event planners, it could help lessen the fear of the task and turn it into fun.

PURPOSE NOTES

PRAYER

O thou that hearest prayer, unto thee shall all flesh come.

—Psalm 65:2

PRAYER

O thou that hearest prayer, unto thee shall all flesh come.
—Psalm 65:2

Who

As a group, your committee should make a commitment to pray for the event you are planning. Whether it's for ten minutes a day or thirty minutes a week, it should be a consistent time devoted solely for the program.

What

Your committee will be praying for each other. That way, you know you will be strengthened and empowered for the tasks that must be completed.

Your committee will pray for the speakers you've chosen. That they will be able to minister to those who have spiritual needs.

Your committee will be praying for the people who will attend. They could be part of the harvest that the Lord wishes to save. Many will never to go to a formal church service, but they will attend a small session. This gives them the opportunity to hear the gospel and to respond to it.

Some will not be able to attend your church's Sunday School. A workshop or seminar might be just what they prefer to encourage them in the Christian walk. We are advised to build each other up in our faith.

Why

Prayer is key. To know God's will and direction, you <u>must</u> pray.

Prayer and Fasting

The more power you wish to see, the more time you should spend in prayer. If you add fasting to it, as a committee, you will see much power evidenced. You will see God move in ways you could never imagine.

Prayer for revival—Psalm 85:6—Wilt thou not revive us again: that thy people may rejoice in thee?

Prayer for harvest—Matt 9:37-38 or Luke 10:2—the harvest truly is great, but the labourers are few; pray ye therefore the Lord of the harvest, that he would send forth labourers into his harvest.

Assurance of answered prayer—1 John 3:21-22—and whatsoever we ask, we receive of him, because we keep his commandments, and do those things that are pleasing in his sight.

PRAYER NOTES

WHAT TYPE OF GATHERING

For where two or three come together in my name, I am there with them.

—Matthew 18:20

WHAT TYPE OF GATHERING

For where two or three come together in my name, I am there with them.

—*Matthew 18:20*

There are at least three types of gatherings: instructional, thematic, and seminar or workshop. This manual is generally organized to help a committee plan a workshop since it requires many of the same elements of preparation and outreach as the others.

In most instances, you really should decide on an overall theme. Perhaps it will come from the larger congregational theme. It should reflect a particular need, which will spark the interest of your audience. Most of the work that you will need to do as a committee in order to plan a workshop will stem from thematic tasks. You will need to know your people to decide how much advertising or outreach your participants will require to generate interest in attending your gathering. Some members attend every year, no matter what. Some members who have never attended, may like to know that they would be welcome to attend.

This manual will also be helpful to you in organizing the process by which you should approach planning your event. Take time to think about the gathering as a whole, not just your curriculum or schedule and what you wish to accomplish.

Seminar:

> - a small group engaged in research under the guidance of a facilitator who meets regularly with them for reports and discussions

> - a course or study so pursued

> - a scheduled meeting of such a group

> - a meeting or an exchange of ideas in certain areas

Workshop:

> - an area, room or establishment in which work is done

> - a group of people who meet regularly for a seminar in a specialized field

Summit:

> - the highest point or part

> - the top of a mountain

> - the highest degree of achievement or status

> - figuratively, summit suggests the highest level attainable

> - peak, the highest point of achievement

Meeting:

- the act or process of coming together, encounter

- an assembly or gathering of people

- agreement

- concord

Conference:

- a meeting for consultation or discussion

- an exchange of views

- a meeting of committees to settle differences

Support Group

- to be capable of bearing each other

- to keep from falling or slipping or yielding during stress

- to provide subsistence

TYPE OF GATHERING NOTES

Your Focus
Your Theme
Your Approach

In the beginning, when God...

—Genesis 1a

YOUR FOCUS
YOUR THEME
YOUR APPROACH

In the beginning, when God...

—Genesis 1a

Your Focus

After you have a general idea about your subject matter, your committee should take some time to brainstorm about the parts of this focus area, which are of interest. Make a list on a board or large paper on an easel so that everyone can see all of the ideas. If you have the time, try to evaluate each part at this point. When your group is satisfied with its effort, you will need to vote on which topic is of utmost important to the general membership. The top three will be your focus.

Your Theme

The committee can now decide on an overall theme that will incorporate the top three parts of the focus.

Your Approach

So now you have your title, your themes, what about how you're going to present all of these great ideas? You will need to decide together on a format for your gathering. *Consider this your approach.*

In general, feedback from past workshops has shown that one of the most consistently highly rated experiences by participants is varying seminars that build on the main theme. This is where participants are allowed to focus more personally on the material or ideas being shared. These sessions are usually facilitated by an experienced group leader, and can have specific agenda. Having small group sessions is key in allowing participants to communicate better.

YOUR FOCUS/APPROACH/THEME NOTES

TEAMWORK

Your Planning Committee

A nation will fall if it has no guidance. Many advisors mean security.

—Proverbs 11:14

YOUR PLANNING COMMITTEE

A nation will fall if it has no guidance. Many advisors mean security.

—Proverbs 11:14

Develop a committee that is comprised of either five or seven people. You can hand pick them or ask for volunteers. These people should be involved in some activity in your church or group. However, it is a good idea to decide together on a chair (for a group of five or seven) or co-chairs (for seven or more). It is helpful to have people fill these roles simply for organizational reasons. If there is more than one person or two who can keep everything together, perhaps who have a little more time to give and/or more experience, it aids in keeping track of completed and future tasks. This does not mean that this person or people will emerge into roles as time goes by. However, it is important to realize that the group should continue to make decisions as a whole. Try your hardest to ensure that the rule of eighty-twenty does not begin to befall you, having twenty percent of the people on your committee doing eighty percent of the work.

Don't even think about trying to avoid conflict in your group. You are going to be working together for months. You're probably going to get stressed out from time to time. People may not live up to their roles. These are all natural things. Managing conflict in your group will only make you stronger—avoiding it will work to pull you apart.

You need to remember most of all that you are working toward the same goal. You all work in ways that are most comfortable for you. If you respect these things, and communicate well, you will do just fine.

Go ahead if you have all your people. If not, here are just a couple of suggestions. Try to make your group diverse. The more ideas, the better—as long as your group can learn to handle discussions and work toward group decision-making. Try to pay attention to the types of workers you have in your group. Get a mix of thinkers. Try to get various people who enjoy being extroverted and who enjoy introversion. Get some task workers and get some big picture people. This will help later when you delegate responsibilities.

The point of this exercise is to help you all begin to share a vision about what the next four or more months will be like. Everyone needs to understand the effort it will take to plan a successful workshop event and everyone must be willing to follow it through to the end.

From now on, you will need to pay close attention to the time you take in your meetings to complete your tasks. Stay on task during your meeting times as much as possible. Your meetings should run between one and two hours depending on debate and workload.

Take some time to have fun. Get out and do something together, lunch or coffee. Go bowling. Plan something around a work holiday. Your meeting time can get crazy, so be sure to allow other times that as a group you can be more social.

PLANNING COMMITTEE NOTES

CREATING A TEAM

People may plan all sorts of things, but the Lord's will is going to be done.

—Proverbs 19:21

CREATING A TEAM

People may plan all sorts of things, but the Lord's will is going to be done.

—Proverbs 19:21

It is important to have a team of leaders with diversities of gifts, talents, passions, and personalities but in the same Spirit. One leader might have the word of discernment, one with the talent of creative expressions or one with the gift of administration. We are reminded in the twelfth chapter of 1 Corinthians that there is not a part of the body that is more important than another part. "If the whole body were hearing, how could we smell?" Remember to look out among your congregation and community and see the willing laborers ready to work for kingdom building.

Working diligently together:	"So we will build the wall, and the entire wall was joined together up to half its height, for the people had the mind to work." Nehemiah 4:6
Iron sharpens iron:	"As iron sharpens iron, so a man sharpens the countenance of his friend." Proverbs 27:17
Teamwork in reaching others:	"I planted, Apollos watered, but God gave the increase." I Cor. 3:6-9

The Gifts	The Person	Their Job
The Eyes of Understanding	VISIONARY	Someone who sees the fullest potential and benefit of convening a conference for women. They come with fresh ideas.
Feeds you with knowledge And understanding	THE GUIDE	Someone who has a heart for people, who cares about what is happening to women globally; who cares about the information being disseminated and looking for positive impacts and results.
Guides you skillfully	ADMINISTRATOR	Someone who gets things done, follows through, and pays attention to details.
Does not withhold any Good thing	ENCOURAGER	Some one who is enthusiastic and a cheerleader about the conference. This person will remind everyone that their strength is in the Lord and all things will work out for the good of those who believe.
A planner and designer	ORGANIZER	This person is not interested in being in charge but will get things done for the glory of God. A great planner is a doer. This person works closely with the Administrator.
Be Spiritually Prepared	PRAYER WARRIOR	A person who will be the foundation of your team, will be ministering to the team and for the team in prayer and encouragement.

CREATING A TEAM NOTES

Formulating A Plan

I alone know the plans I have toward you, plans to bring you prosperity and not disaster, plans to bring about the future you hope for.

—Jeremiah 29:11

FORMULATING A PLAN

I alone know the plans I have toward you, plans to bring you prosperity and not disaster; plans to bring about the future you hope for.

—Jeremiah 29:11

Pretend that the only ideas about planning a gathering that you have are the ones you alone or each of one of your committee already have. In order to include everyone in the planning process, you should brainstorm about all of the things you should do to plan a gathering. Have a member of the group write everything down as you go. Remember the rules of brainstorming:

- there are no bad ideas,
- nothing is evaluated either verbally or non-verbally,
- say everything that pops into your head out loud,
- write everything down.

Keep each idea on a separate piece of paper (post-its work well). After the group is satisfied with its effort to brainstorm, place all of the notes on the table for everyone to see. An alternative method would be to number them by vote count. The group, without speaking, should arrange the notes in the order in which they believe the tasks should be completed. The group must be in consensus, silently, before they are allowed to speak. At this point, the group may assemble a list, in order, of the tasks ahead.

We suggest that the next thing you all do is to look through the manual, at least the table of contents and the "Timeline" page and see if you've missed anything. Compare your lists and make any adjustments necessary.

Your group should now make a compiled list of expectations. After you are satisfied with the completion of your list, talk about the expectations. Make sure that everyone who wants to continue on the committee is willing to try to live up to them. If someone feels they will not be able to remain on the committee, make an effort to retain them, but if it is not feasible, ask the individual to suggest a replacement.

From now on, you will need to pay close attention to the time you take in your meetings to complete you tasks. Attempt to keep your meetings as short as possible so that everyone will be willing to attend knowing the meeting will not last two or three hours. Your meetings should not run more than one hour and a half, depending on the discussion and the items on the agenda to be covered for that meeting.

FORMULATING A PLAN NOTES

DATE

Everything that happens in this world happens at the time God chooses.

—Ecclesiastes 3:1

DATE

Everything that happens in this world happens at the time God chooses.

—*Ecclesiastes 3:1*

One of the most crucial decisions that you will make is to decide on a date. For an instructional gathering, this is perhaps not as crucial since you will probably require people to be there. However, if you are in any way trying to solicit participation, you seriously need to think about this step in the initial planning process.

In conjunction with deciding the date, you need to think about how much time your event will span. Conferences can last anywhere from a day to a week. One important thing for you to consider is that whatever you decide on length of time will effect the type of approach you use in the presentation of the material. Keep in mind that it is a good idea to allow for small group experiences in addition to the time you need for presentation of your program. Your selection of length of your gathering will also depend on your budget. For example, you may be able to afford a half-day gathering, or a two- or three-day conference. You need to be thinking about this as you decide your time frame. Your choice of location needs to take into account your budget, time of year, the size of your group, and type of accommodations you desire.

Check the church's calendar to see if your date will conflict with other major events with prior history. You wouldn't want your program to happen just before "the church's anniversary", for example, if many of your invitees will be working on that.

THE DATE NOTES

TIMELINE

Everything that happens in this world happens at the time God chooses.

—Ecclesiastes 3:1

TIMELINE

Everything that happens in this world happens at the time God chooses.

—Ecclesiastes 3:1

A timeline will really help your committee plan for the rest of the time and the tasks that you have to do. If you have not read through the rest of this manual yet, now is a good time to do it. You need to read all the way through the end in order to understand not only the big things that are left to be done, but the details too. You could assign that detailed-oriented person on your committee these tasks. The "big picture" individual can handle the overall scope of the event.

Next, take out a large, poster-size piece of paper and draw out the next two months day by day. Leave plenty of room to write down specific tasks and empty space to fill in things that come up along the way. It's a good idea to post it on the wall of a room where all of the committee will see it regularly. If this is not possible, perhaps a person on the committee can be responsible for the calendar or, if one person has access to a computer, they could develop a spreadsheet and hand it out to each member.

Mark the big event on the poster, then work backward, listing each task and what date you wish to see it accomplished.

TIMELINE NOTES

MONEY

If one of you is planning to build a tower, he sits down and figures out what it will cost, to see if he has enough money to finish the job.

—Luke 14:2

MONEY

If one of you is planning to build a tower, he sits down first and figures out what it will cost, to see if he has enough money to finish the job.

—Luke 14:2

The most straightforward way to deal with figuring out your budget is to consider first your gathering site cost—it will most likely be your largest expense. Keep in mind that you can charge your participants nothing, all, or part of the cost of attending your conference or workshop. However, if you are requiring as many participants as possible to be there, you should consider covering most of this cost yourselves as there will be some who simply cannot afford it.

An excellent way to deal with the cost of planning and executing a gathering is to look at the church-wide annual budget allowance for your auxiliary. There may be some funds allocated for special contingencies.

One great method is to solicit private donations from the membership.

Another suggestion is to consider donations from the general congregation. Ask the leaders of your church for permission to have a special offering taken, and be sure to make an announcement to the congregation what it will be used for.

Alternatively, plan to charge each participant a small amount, enough to cover all your expenses, or an amount to cover your expenses, plus a bit more to put in a fund for the following year if you plan to do this conference annually. Or, just enough to cover the cost of the food and beverages.

Make sure you estimate what you will have to pay, if anything, for the meeting space and any refreshments. If members will be coming from out of town, how will their expenses be handled? Get approval from your group for the budget. Find and reserve an affordable place to hold the event. Keep in mind how many people you think will attend and how many rooms you will need to have for workshops.

Other costs to consider include printing, copying your facilitators' materials, pens, markers, flip charts, mileage reimbursement for your speakers, speaker honorariums, extra food, postage for mass mailings, phone bills, and money to take your committee out for lunch after the event is complete if you can manage it.

When you have finished estimating costs for each of these items, list them one by one on a tally page. Then, list your projected revenue. If you come out on the plus side, you're doing great. If, however, you are short, you will have to figure out where you can find some more money.

It is important to deal with the budget right away. Fully understand how much you will have to work with so you won't have to go into debt and be unable to pay the bills.

Lastly, be sure to keep records. A person should be responsible for collecting all receipts from the committee and making sure that you all are not over-spending.

Solicitation

One way you may be able to solicit support for your event is through asking for gifts-in-kind. Gifts-in-kind are essentially contributions; free of liability, planning obligation, or reciprocation. Often, corporations are allotted a certain amount of money and/or resources they may donate throughout the year. For example, a bookstore may give you pens, Coca-Cola may be able to give you some free beverages, a grocery store may give you breakfast rolls, etc. The liability, planning obligation, or reciprocation. Often, corporations are allotted a certain amount of money and/or resources they may donate throughout the year. For example, a bookstore may give you pens, Coca-Cola may be able to give you some free beverages, a grocery store may give you breakfast rolls, etc.

The best way to approach receiving gifts-in-kind is to call to get the name of the store manager or individual who makes the decision to donate to charitable organizations. Then write a letter explaining your event, the date and what you'd like their particular store or corporation to provide any part or all. Decide what you plan to offer your attendees, whether a continental breakfast, mid-morning fruit, rolls and coffee, lunch, or a mid-afternoon snack. You will need to provide in sufficient quantities for the number of people who have registered. Decide what you will need (on which you might be able to save a significant amount of money without having to provide it yourselves), then call different companies and ask for their support.

Start planning for this process when you do your budget. You may want to make some calls at that time to receive verbal commitments of support. However, the actual time to negotiate contributions should be started at five weeks out and end with enough time to receive and adjust to donations.

Remember to mention during the event those who gave generously or print in your program the persons or businesses who donated funds and/or products.

MONEY NOTES

SPEAKERS/ FACILITATORS

When wise people speak, they make knowledge attractive.

—Proverbs 15:2

If you know what you are talking about, you have something more valuable than gold or jewels.

—Proverbs 20:15

SPEAKERS/FACILITATORS

When wise people speak, they make knowledge attractive.

—*Proverbs 15:2*

If you know what you are talking about, you have something more valuable than gold or jewels.

—*Proverbs 20:15*

Many women's committees organize a women's gathering every year or every other year. A women's conference typically lasts a day or a day and a half and features speakers from the area.

A gathering can be an excellent way to provide training and get the group focused on issues of concern to women members. Gatherings, however, take a lot of advance planning and hard work on the part of the women's committee. Don't be discouraged if your first gathering is relatively small. If you plan well-organized, useful gatherings, they will develop a great reputation and attendance will grow.

We've covered:

• the timeline

• deciding a theme or purpose

• setting a date that doesn't conflict with holidays or other church functions

• developing a realistic budget for the gathering.

Now, the time has come to make a decision about whether or not to use guest speakers or presenters. This decision is one that you all as a committee should make together. Using outside people is a good way to increase the diversity of your group, expose your people to new ideas, and inform them about topics which you may or may not be able to address yourselves from a personal perspective. Of course, speakers widely vary in their abilities to motivate, entertain, and inform an audience. Ask the group or others you know about a speaker's reputation and impressions.

Determine what workshop topics you want to offer and how many workshops you want to have. Select and invite workshop facilitators. If you decide to use outside speakers, you will need to start contacting them a little over two months out. If they are well known, you will need to contact them as early as six months, if you really want that person to participate. Do not wait until the last minute to start finding people for your event. It is difficult to line up all of your first choice speakers simply because of scheduling. It is even more difficult to come up with alternate speakers and coordinate all of their schedules. You need to have several back-up plans in this area—not only first and second choice speakers, but alternative ideas for presenting your material if you cannot find available presenters.

It might be a good idea to try for at least one "big name" person to speak at your gathering. It can do wonders in recruiting participants to be able to tell them that "the author of whatever" will be there. Aim high, you have nothing to lose.

If you know other people or organizations that have used speakers in the past, ask to see the evaluations. Pay attention to specific comments that were made by participants and facilitators. Ask people in the organization, if they are still around, if they think the presenter would be qualified to speak on the topics for which you are looking.

When speakers confirm with you, send them a confirmation letter right away, reiterating what you talked about on the telephone. Ask them to send you a short biography (you provide the format, if possible) back when they receive it in the letter. You will need this information later when you put together your materials for publicity and it's a hassle to have to call everyone back. In the letter, thank them for accepting your invitation, review the topic in detail on which you have asked them to speak, send them complete address and directions to the location to your event site. If they are not familiar with the area, a map would be helpful. Tell them where to park and where a committee member will meet them. Tell them the time that their session will begin and end. If you know which room they have been assigned, you could include that. You may also want to ask them to let you know if they will need any special materials for their presentations. You may need to re-arrange your schedule a little depending on the speaker's availability. If this happens, you will need to revisit your schedule and nail it down in its adjusted form.

SPEAKERS/FACILITATORS NOTES

Advertising

The news spread about him through the whole country of Syria so that people brought to him all those who were sick, suffering from all kinds of diseases and disorders.

—Matthew 4:24

ADVERTISING

The news spread about him through the whole country of Syria so that people brought to him all those who were sick, suffering from all kinds of diseases and disorders.

—*Matthew 4:24*

You will need to start to develop the materials you will use for advertising and outreach at least seven weeks before the event. By this, we mean the creation of the posters, flyers, radio script, brochure, and ads for the church monthly newsletter and weekly bulletin. They will need to be in every Sunday's bulletin to get people interested. Also, whenever a member of the committee attends another meeting, they should politely ask if they could announce the event.

At six weeks out, you should have the materials in distribution. Advertising and outreach will be a big part of your event planning process if you are planning a thematic or workshop-type gathering. You may still want to develop outreach materials, however. It may be helpful for the people you are asking to attend to have an idea of what they can expect at your event. As soon as it's final, providing a schedule is always a good idea.

Try to think of every possible way you can reach people, and get your materials out with plenty of time in advance of your event (at least one month before registration begins). People generally need to hear about something several times before it starts to sound like a good idea. Still, the best way to attract people to an event is through positive word of mouth. Unfortunately, for a new program, this doesn't usually work very well. Just try to have a positive attitude about what you have planned regardless of the number of people you get to come. Your programming is something on which you have worked hard. If your numbers are low and going to apparently stay that way, try to not get too discouraged. It takes a long time to build tradition and involvement.

Making Your Brochure, Flyers & Posters

The best way to make this easy on yourself, depending on your budget, is to have someone else do them. However, if you have a computer, a printer, and an ability to enlarge to poster size (either on your own or through a copying center), you can do this yourself. Prepare a registration form and determine how you will get it out to members. You may want to include a list of workshops and ask people to pre-register.

Try to print all of your outreach and advertising materials in the same color and/or with some kind of recognizable symbol on everything. People will begin to associate the flyer to the right program the more consistent that you are. You don't have to get fancy. You just need to get them recognized. Use something flashy on posters and flyers. They are intended to grab the attention of the person walking by. If you have too much detail in these items, they will not be read. Save the more detailed information for your brochure.

Brochures should include a purpose statement, a schedule, a registration slip, and general information about your specific event (be this speakers or themes or location).

If the speaker attends another church or is the leader of an organization, provide them with a supply of the advertising flyers. Ask them to invite their families and friends as well.

Distribution of Brochures, Flyers & Posters

The basic idea here is that you will need to cover as much ground as humanly possible. You need to actively distribute information to a diversity of auxiliaries. Send and/or deliver your materials to the leader as well as a personalized invitation. You should send information, use e-mail, and use the phone. The more ways you let people know about your event, the better. Radio stations and some television stations will also run ads for churches and non-profit organizations at no cost.

ADVERTISING NOTES

Developing Your Materials

No speech or words are used, no sound is heard, yet their voice goes out to all the world and is heard to the ends of the earth...

—Psalm 19:3-4a

DEVELOPING YOUR MATERIALS

No speech or words are used, no sound is heard; yet their voice goes out to all the world and is heard to the ends of the earth...
                                                    —*Psalm 19:3-4a*

Materials are everything you will give your facilitators and committee members so they know what's going on all the time, and what you will give your participants for the same reason. This should include: your schedule, topic, speaker, and speaker biography, and any handouts you will give them to use during the gathering; and optional other information.

The participant materials should be given to them on the way to or first thing at the gathering site. The facilitator materials should be given to them at their first session and left with them to review before the event.

The facilitator materials include all the information they wish to be used in their session. You should budget for the printing costs and make sure you will have a sufficient number of copies for each participant for each workshop.

As your event approaches, you will need to double-check all assigned tasks. You may feel it necessary to call your speakers, just to touch base to be sure they are ready and to let them know that you have provided their handouts and any audio-visual aids they may need for their presentations.

Have a speaker meeting. You will need to introduce the committee and the speakers will get to meet each other. Promote a short discussion about your mutual expectations in accordance with the theme for the gathering. It is also important to provide time for the facilitators to get to know each other.

Determine all the supplies you will need to bring and/or provide for the event. This may include pens, markers, flip charts, paper, notebooks, treats, and drinks. It's a good idea to assign specific supplies to different people on your committee for them to remember. Decide if you will have small gifts for the participants.

Decide on the timing for your opening session, who will introduce the speaker to the rest of the group at the beginning of each workshop. Work out your gathering closure, whether you will want to have closing remarks, a prayer, a time of testimony and who might lead it. Get all your supplies, purchase the food for the meal or snacks you've planned. Each committee member should complete their list of *everything* she is responsible for bringing.

Make sure that each workshop room is set up as you want it to be. The podium is in place, there are enough chairs, the microphone works, the lighting and temperature are good, the handouts are ready, the AV equipment is set up.

Assign people to greet your incoming speakers. You will need to make sure that the speakers know which room they will be in and that everything they've requested is in place. Ask committee members to be trouble-shooters for any problems that may arise.

Make sure that all of your materials are current. If you had changes in speakers, you need to add the new biographies. Make sure you have extra copies of the schedule and it is printed correctly. Make sure you've made adjustments for late registrants.

DEVELOPING YOUR MATERIALS NOTES

DELEGATE

Jesus called the twelve disciples together and gave them power and authority to drive out all demons and to cure diseases.

—Luke 9:11

DELEGATE

Jesus called the twelve disciples together and gave them power and authority to drive out all demons and to cure diseases.

—*Luke 9:11*

The best thing that you can do is to make sure that you delegate among the committee the rest of the tasks to be done. A printed timeline for each member, with their name next to their task might be in order. The major things that you need to do from here on out are:

a) getting speakers;

b) advertising and outreach;

c) registration and administration of participant information;

d) creation of all materials for facilitators and participants,

e) facilitator training, if needed;

f) soliciting gifts-in-kind, (i.e., food/beverages/paper products, etc.) and,

g) last minute confirmations and organization of details of your event.

One of the easiest ways is to divide tasks is to evaluate and recognize each other's interests and strengths. If "April" is very detail oriented, likes to work on a computer and doesn't much care for talking on the phone, you would not want her to be in charge of advertising and outreach. Instead, a good job for "April" might be development of facilitator and participant materials.

You need to be very deliberate in making sure that the tasks that are left are evenly divided among the committee. This is the time in the planning process when things can start to get a little crazy. If individuals try to take on too many tasks, stress levels could potentially be unhealthy here. You will need to monitor each other as a committee from here on out to ensure that people are working on the tasks they are supposed to be, and that no one is bearing an enormous brunt of the work.

You should all be responsible for distributing advertising and outreach materials, and soliciting gifts-in-kind. Distribute the registration form and gathering information throughout the church. Use auxiliary meetings, newsletters and the church network to get the materials out. As the date draws closer, you should plan to advertise more heavily to generate interest and excitement.

This does not imply that these tasks do not need coordinators. Once people get rolling on each of these jobs, you will need to have a person in charge of each of them to assemble information and finalize engagements.

Try to remember one of the most important things about group work: 20% of the people usually do 80% of the work. Try not to let this happen, it's way too stressful for everybody.

DELEGATE NOTES

REGISTRATION

Everyone, then, went to register himself, each to his own hometown.

—Luke 2:3

REGISTRATION

Everyone, then, went to register himself, each to his own home-town.

—Luke 2:3

The registration process should start at three weeks out from your event date and end the week before the event. This will allow you time to give a final head count for the gathering and to take care of any scheduling issues with group and room assignments. You will also know how much food and/or snacks to purchase and prepare. Regardless of which type of gathering you are planning, you will need to have some form of notification of the registration dates and process. The decision should be made now as to which room will hold the greatest number of people and assign the workshop to the room with the largest number of registrants. It is generally a good idea to set the start and end dates of registration. Most people will wait until the last possible day to register, so having it set with time left for you to adjust is essential.

One tool that you can use in controlling the numbers of participants at your event is to set the number of registration forms to be accepted ahead of time. You may say that the first twenty-five people will have a spot and after that, registration is full. There are pros and cons to this approach. For a popular event, it makes those who really want to attend get out and do it early. For an event, which may be popular, it gives the public the illusion that you will be filling quickly. This can convince people that your gathering is a good thing to do, and it can scare people away who usually do things at the last minute.

Having unlimited numbers leaves you open to taking as many participants as your site can accommodate. Monitor the process, know the maximum number of people you can accommodate, and adjust your recruitment efforts accordingly during the two weeks of registration. Keep in mind, most people wait until the last minute to sign up. Also, you will always have some that miss the date, you should have a backup plan as to how you will deal with them. If you have unlimited space, you will not have to take this in consideration.

If you are charging your participants, you will need to have a secured method for collecting funds at the time they register. You may choose to have the same price charged throughout registration, or you can stack the price for up-front enrollment. (For example, charge $10 the first week and $15 the second.) It works best to have registration in one location, at least handled by one person on your committee. Create a file as you go with participant information. Have hard copies of the registration forms and if you can, enter the names of the participants in an Excel file or similar program on computer. Be sure to keep track of whether or not they have paid.

Distribute post-registration materials at the time of every participant's registration.

REGISTRATION NOTES

CHECKLIST

Whosoever is wise and will observe these things, even they shall understand the loving kindness of the Lord.

—Psalm 107:43

CHECKLIST

Whosoever is wise and will observe these things, even they shall understand the loving kindness of the Lord.

—*Psalm 107:43*

Reducing your level of stress while you are in the planning stages depends as much on strong organizational skills as it does on good people skills. It is easy to get sidetracked by day to day demands, so it is crucial to prioritize your tasks for the gathering. Always keep the goal insight.

The resources listed below will steer you toward additional information and useful tools that can make your planning more productive and stress free.

- Keep a master to do list and refer to it every day.

- Invest the time necessary to organize your work.

- Complete at least one task each day that will take you toward your long-term goals.

- Reward yourself and other committee members when you reach interim goals and deadlines.

- Take breaks to clear your mind and it will give you more energy to finish your work.

- Schedule a lunch with a friend or two who are on the committee to gain new perspectives on planning situations.

- Delegate responsibilities where appropriate, to others who can free you for higher-priority assignments.

To Do Master List
Too Little Time, Too Much to Do? Prioritize!

Task:	Must Do	Should Do	Could Do	Want to Do

Project Planning Worksheet
Managing Tasks Efficiently

Keeping the gathering projects on time and on track requires absolute clarity about who does what, when, and in which order. Use this form to assist you.

Task:
Participant:

Task Start Date:
Task End Date:

Task
Description:

Who does it:

Phone:

E-mail:
What to do before each task?

What to do after each task?

Start Date:

End Date:

Ways To Make Committee Meetings Productive

Time invested in preparing for a meeting will pay off in a focused discussion that accomplishes the agenda in record time. If you are running the meeting, follow these pointers to keep it on track.

> Invite only the key people involved.

> Circulate an agenda several days before the meeting date and give a deadline for attendees' feedback.

> Set a time limit for each agenda item and stick to it.

> Assign each agenda item to a person who will be responsible for it.

> Bring pen, paper, and your appointment book to the meeting so you can note any essential information.

> Assign someone to take minutes.

> Always start the meeting right on time, even if some people haven't yet arrived.

> Allow each person a set amount of time to speak.

> Try to involve everyone attending. Ask questions of someone who's not contributing.

> If the purpose of the meeting is to have a brainstorming session, make a rule that no one can shoot down an idea.

> Focus on making decisions rather than simply continuing discussion.

> Table for another meeting any topics that aren't on the agenda.

> Make sure that the minutes detail the commitments agreed to, and distribute a copy of the minutes to all who attended.

> After each meeting, ask yourself how you could have run it more smoothly if there were any problems.

The committee members will appreciate meetings that start on time and end on time and accomplish the agenda for the time allotted.

CHECKLIST NOTES

COUNTDOWN

And Jacob served seven years for Rachel; and they seemed to him but a few days, for the love he had to her.

—Genesis 29:20

COUNTDOWN

And Jacob served seven years for Rachel; and they seemed to him but a few days, for the love he had to her.

—Genesis 29:20

One Year to Six Months Ahead:

- Set a date for the gathering that doesn't conflict with holidays or other functions.

- Develop a realistic budget.

- Decide if you will charge a registration fee

- Get approval for the budget.

- Find and reserve an affordable place to hold the gathering.

- Decide on a theme for the gathering.

- Pray

Three to Four Months Ahead:

- Determine what topics you want to offer and how many workshops you want to have.
- Decide on speakers and send invitation letters

Two Months Ahead:

- Start publicizing the gathering.
- Follow up with the invited speakers
- Prepare registration forms. If you are collecting a fee, determine who will be in charge.

One Month Ahead:

- Continue to advertise.
- Start working on the program, including the times for each workshop and the location if known.
- Let the speakers know any important details.
- Pray

One to Two Weeks Before:

- Confirm with each speaker. Let them know you've made the arrangements for their audio-visual needs. Ask if they will require anything they may have forgotten.
- Confirm arrangements with the facility.
- Adjust the number of chairs, configuration of the rooms, amount of food based on the numbers of registrations received.
- Assemble participant packets.
- Print the program.
- Make sure you will have enough food.

The Day Before:

- Make sure all materials and supplies are ready to be copied.
- Pray

The Day of the Conference:

- Arrive at the facility early to confirm that everything is as you requested.
- Have water available for each speaker.
- Assign a committee member to greet speakers
- Assign committee members to greet participants and hand out packets.
- Make sure speakers' handouts are in sufficient quantity for the number of participants in each workshop.

After the Gathering:

- Make sure all rented equipment is returned.
- Pay any outstanding bills; make a summary of the income and expenses.
- Write thank-you letters to speakers, workshop leaders, and everyone else who helped.
- Do a summary of the workshop evaluations.

COUNTDOWN NOTES

Making It Yours

No farmer goes on constantly plowing his fields and getting them ready for planting. Once he has prepared the soil, he plants the seeds.

—Isaiah 28:24-25

MAKING IT YOURS

No farmer goes on constantly plowing his fields and getting them
ready for planting. Once he has prepared the soil, he plants the
seeds.

—Isaiah 28:24-25

Christian women have always sought to reach out to each other in good times and especially in bad times. Gatherings, conferences, or workshops have traditionally been a helpful method to provide opportunities for women to learn and to use various tools and techniques for self-reflection in areas such as personal empowerment, strengthening relationships with God, and with each other.

How you make the gathering yours is by assessing the needs of your people. You may wish to talk to a few friends and ask them if a gathering with the topics you have in mind would be beneficial to them. Or, you may wish to keep it within the circle of the committee.

Keep in mind your objectives. There should be at least three things the participant should gain from attending the workshop.

One, the participant should develop and focus on strategies to improve intrapersonal and interpersonal skills. The focus question: what do I need to do differently in my life to accomplish my goal in life?

Two, the participant should develop a list of ideas and methods to connect more positively with intergeneration wisdom.

Three, the participant should write, listen, and partake in discussions or activities that will encourage growth in new areas.

Additionally, the participant should feel comfortable in a non-threatening atmosphere to give them a sense of completion and accomplishment.

Think of workshops you may have attended. Think of the good things you came away with that improved your walk with the Lord.

MAKING IT YOURS NOTES

Evaluations

And above all, take the shield of faith, so that you will be able to quench all the fiery darts of the wicked.

—Ephesians 6:16

EVALUATIONS

And above all, take the shield of faith, so that you will be able to quench all the fiery darts of the wicked.

—*Ephesians 6:16*

Before you send out your thank you letters, you should design, print and hand out evaluations at each workshop. Someone should be in charge of collecting them at the close of the workshop. Tally up your evaluations from the gathering. This shouldn't take more that a couple of hours. It is a good idea to save the tabulated results for the next planning committee meeting (and it's a good idea to have one within a month after the conference). Evaluations should be a combination of both quantitative and qualitative data (i.e. comments and scales of satisfaction measured numerically).

EVALUTATIONS NOTES

THANK YOU LETTERS

In everything give thanks for this is the will of God in Christ Jesus, concerning you.

—1 Thessalonians 5:18

THANK YOU LETTERS

In everything give thanks for this is the will of God in Christ Jesus, concerning you.

—*1 Thessalonians 5:18*

You will need to write thank you letters (or send a card) to all of your committee members, your facilitators, your speakers, and especially your sponsors. When you send thanks to the speakers and the small group facilitators, it is a good idea to include a letter to them with the results and comments of their evaluations. Don't forget the building manager, the custodial service, and security personnel if appropriate. If you plan to hold a seminar each year, they will look kindly on your event.

THANK YOU LETTERS NOTES

Appendix

APPENDIX

Sample Forms:

Flyer

Topic Ideas

Survey Of Needs/Concerns

Calendar

Timeline

Letter to church auxiliaries

Letter to the Senior Pastor

Letter of Invitation to the Speaker

Letter of Confirmation to the Speaker

Pointers for Speaker Success

AV Equipment Request Form

Registration

Workshop Evaluation Form

Thank you Letter

Recipe

WOMEN'S CONFERENCE FLYER

Don't miss this opportunity to fellowship, share and pray with your Sisters in Christ. This will take place [day, month], 200X at _____. The seminar will begin with a continental breakfast which includes a time of praise and worship.

Teaching by different Godly women will encourage you to grow in your personal relationship as you see how God has equipped the lives of women just like you.

For more information contact:

XXXXXX

XXXXXX

Call (XXX) XXX-XXXX

WHEN WOMEN GATHER CONFERENCE

Sample Ideas—Topics for Workshops

Index Guide	Topics	Reference(s)
Abilities	Invest your wisely	Mt. 13:12-13, 25:15
	Using your gifts in the church	Acts 6:2-4, Eph.4:4-7
Abundance	Don't forget God in your abundance	Dt. 8:11-19
Bargaining	Keeping your end of a bargain	Gn. 29:28-30
	Gideon bargaining with God?	Jdg.6:37
Basic of Faith	Never forget	2 Pt. 1:12-15, 1 Jn. 2:24
Caring	Let others know you care for them	Rom. 1:6-9
Cross	What it means to "take up your cross"	Mt. 10:38, Mt. 16:24, Mk 8:34, Lk.14:27
Debts/Debtors	Dealing with our debts Why is love for others called a Debt?	Prv. 3:27-28 Rom. 13:1-10
Encouragement	Reviewing past blessings	Jos. 24: 2-13
Faith	What is it? Tested when we face Difficulties; becomes strong in face of opposition Strengthening by waiting	Lk. 17:6 Gn. 12:10-13 Jdgs 3:28-30 Mt. 9:27-30
Gifts	God uses whatever gifts you have Salvation is a gift from God	Acts 9:36-42 Jn 3:8

Sample Ideas—Topics on Women in the Bible

Man's helper	Genesis 2:18
Women without inheritance	Genesis 31:15-16
Miriam's song	Exodus 15:21
Daughters who had no brother	Numbers 27:1-11
Asking for favor	Judges 1:13-15
Spoils for conqueror	Judges 5:30
Good Daughter-in-law worth seven sons	Ruth 4:13-15
Evil woman	1 Kings 19:1-2
Prophetess counseled king	2 Chronicles 34:22-28
Queen influence over king	Esther 9:12
Queen's wisdom	Daniel 5:10-11
Women who traveled with Jesus	Luke 8:1-3
Daughters with gift of prophecy	Acts 21:9
Ministry of aged widow	Luke 2:36-38
Sacrifice of a daughter	Judges 11:30-40
Women's questions in early church	1Corinthians 14:34-35
Two quarrelling women	Philippians 4:2

When Women Gather Conference
Sample form
Survey of Needs/Concerns
(Can be used for planning workshops)

What are the top five concerns of Christian Women in the
21st Century?

Check only seven:

Getting an education
Developing friendships with other women
Developing health relationship with men
Desire for spiritual growth
Raising children to be godly
Reaching family goals
Violence against women
Decision-making strategies
Money Matters
Enriching your Health
Single life
Success in the work place
Understanding the Bible
Leadership skills
Enhancing your Self Esteem

Timeline

Months 8-9:

Before the gathering/conference: the organizing committee reports the schedule of future events within the church as well as other churches in the area that might affect the gathering. Choose a date based on this information.

Month 7:

The preliminary program is discussed and decided.

Month 6:

Search for qualified speakers/presenters. Secure their services.

Month 3-5:

Continue to work on the program. Confirm the reservations with the facility. Continue to solicit funding and/or donations of goods.

Months 2-0:

Publicize the event. Let the participant start thinking they should not miss the event and have time to put it on their schedule.

Deadline for registration: if a fee is being charged, encourage participants not to wait until the last minute.

Whatever the deadlines, remember that some participants may decide at the last minute to attend. Be prepared to deal with these changes.

<u>Scripture/Theme</u>

WORKSHOP EVALUATION

Name of Workshop: _____

Facilitator(s): _____

1. How would you rate this workshop?   (1) fair _____
    (2) good _____   (3) excellent _____

2. Did you get what you wanted from this workshop? (Please explain)
    _____

3. What suggestion(s) do you have for improving the Women's Ministries Workshops?
    _____

4. Would you be interested in attending a single (a continuation of this) workshop later in the year?   Yes   No
    If Yes, what day / night would be best? _____

5. Other Comments: _____
    _____
    _____
    _____

(Please use the back if you need more room.)

<u>OPTIONAL:</u>
Please complete the following if you are interested in being on the Workshop committee next year:

Name: _____   Phone No. (   ) _____

Address/Zip/Email: _____

Letter to church auxiliaries

Sample letter to church auxiliaries that will support the event such as Tape Ministry, the Building Manager who schedules the rooms, Security, etc.

Date

Tape Ministry

Re: Women's Week of Workshops

Hello,

The Workshop Committee respectfully requests audiotaping on the following dates:

Wednesday, (date), 7 p.m.
Thursday, (date), 7 p.m.
Friday, (date), 9 a.m. to 3 p.m. (six sessions); each session would last approximately 90 minutes.

We are wondering if we can offer the tapes by pre-order. Also, can the Committee receive any excess funds (after Tape Ministry expenses) to put into an account for next year's workshops?

If you have any questions, feel free to call: _____, at
_____(h); _____ (w); or _____
(email).

Sincerely,

The Workshop Committee

Letter to the Senior Pastor

Sample letter to the Senior Pastor of the church

Date

_____

_____ Church

_____

Dear Reverend _____:

The theme for the Women's Ministry of _____ Church
is_____ _____ _____." {Scripture here}

You are invited and welcome to attend any or all of the workshops.

Friday, {date}, we are scheduling workshops during the day. A continental breakfast will be served at 8:30 a.m. The first two workshops
begin at 9:00 and end at 10:30. The next two begin at 10:45 until
12:15. A light lunch will be served. At 1:30, the last two workshops
begin and the closing session begins at 2:45.

If you have any questions, feel free to call (committee leader) at
_____ or (alternate) at .

Sincerely,

Letter of Invitation to the Speaker

Date

Dear   :

The theme for the Women's Ministry of _____
Church is, "_____ _____." {*Scripture here*}

Our goal is for every woman who attends the Women's week this year
to come away with tools to implement the power of God, enabling
them, their loved ones, and all they may encounter, to live a life of
peace. The Workshop Committee is planning an exciting program and
we are inviting you to prayerfully consider presenting the following session:

"   ", at (time), (day), (month), (year). The presentation
will:
    present the theme of the workshop
    format is 60% participation and 40% direct instruction
    allow last ten minutes for questions, assessment, and evaluation.

A continental breakfast will be served at 8:30 a.m. The first two workshops will begin at 9:00 and end at 10:30 a.m.. The next two begin at
10:45 and end at 12:15 p.m.. A light lunch will be served. At 1:30, the
last two workshops begin and the closing session begins at 2:45 p.m.

We are requesting a short biography, 50-75 words, to use for publicity,
which may be sent by fax to _____, {home} or by mail,
_____.

If you have any questions, feel free to call {committee leader} at
_____ {home phone} or _____ {alternate} at
_____ {home phone}.

Sincerely,

_____ Church Women's Workshop Committee

Letter of Confirmation to the Speaker

    Sample letter to speaker(s) that will attend the event.

Date

Dear   :

Thank you for agreeing to assist in this event! We are excited that you will be able to participate. A meeting with the other speakers and the Gathering Committee will be scheduled two or three weeks prior to the date. You will receive a call to remind you of the date, place and time.

We are requesting a short biography, 50-75 words, to use for publicity, which may be sent by fax to _____, {home} or by mail, _____. Your specific session time will be:

If you have any questions, feel free to call {committee leader} at _____ {home phone} or _____ {alternate} at _____ {home phone}.

Sincerely,

_____ Church Women's Ministries Workshop Committee

Form for Speaker Success

Pointers for A Polished Presentation

Preparing the Talk
Decide on the goal of your presentation and write down your central theme.
Organize your points logically.
Think of personal anecdotes or humorous stories engage your audience from the start.
Tailor the speech to the age, gender and profession of your audience.
Think of rhetorical questions you can ask to get your audience involved.
Use testimony, studies, and statistics to prove your point.
Plan visual aids to supplement your presentation.
Think about questions, especially the difficult ones, your audience is likely to ask, and plan how you'll respond.
Videotape your presentation for review, or practice in front of a good friend who can offer constructive criticism.

Giving the Talk
Arrive early to set up everything and to test any equipment you'll be using.
Introduce your topic so the audience knows what to expect.
Make eye contact with members of the audience.
Speak quickly enough that you hold the audience's interest but slowly enough that they can absorb the material.
Stand up straight.
Speak to your audience. Don't read from note cards or visual aids.
Be lively and energetic.
Summarize your points to leave your audience with the key issues.
Allow adequate time in your presentation to answer questions.
If you don't know the answer to a question, promise to find out.

AV Equipment Request Form

PRESENTER NAME:

DATE NEEDED:

EQUIPMENT REQUESTED

The _____ (church) Workshop Committee is requesting that you fill out the equipment you will need for your workshop. The following materials and equipment are available for the workshop.

	Yes	**No**

VCR

Overhead Projector

Easel (how many)

Markers

Pens, Pencil, Paper

Podium

Xerox Copies of Materials

Other

Sample Registration Form

Sample form—CONFERENCE COST

Per Person

Early Registration $00.00 by Month, Date, 200X

Regular Registration $000.00 after Month Date, 200X

Registration costs paid to When Women Gather Conference include attendance at meetings and workshops, Friday and Saturday Breakfast, Saturday Evening Meal, Sunday Continental Breakfast, and a gift. All other meals are on You.

Official registration time will begins at 4:00 p.m. on Month, Day, 200X

All questions regarding the Conference should be directed to WWGC/ Contact Person. Payments can be mailed to:

XXXXXXX
XXXXXXX
XXXXXXX

Workshop Evaluation Sample Forms

_____CHURCH
WOMEN'S MINISTRIES WORKSHOPS
Date

SCRIPTURE/THEME

WORKSHOP EVALUATION

Name of Workshop:

Facilitator(s):

1. How would you rate this workshop?   (1) fair   (2) good
    (3) excellent

2. Did you get what you wanted from this workshop? (Please explain)

3. What suggestion(s) do you have for improving the Women's Ministries Workshops?

4. Would you be interested in attending a single (a continuation of this) workshop later in the year?   Yes   No
    If Yes, what day/night would be best?

5. Other Comments:

(Please use the back if you need more room.)

OPTIONAL:
Please complete the following if you are interested in being on the Workshop committee next year:

Name: Phone No. (   )

Address/Zip/Email:

When Women Gather Conference
Sample Form-Evaluation for Workshop/Seminar

Workshop Title
Workshop Provider
Date
Time

Please rate the following items

0-not applicable	1
Low	2-3
Medium	4
High	5

Instructor/Presenter

1. Overall quality of the instruction (was a clear, concise method of presentation used)

2. Overall instructor knowledge (your confidence in the instructor's expertise)

3. Use of teaching aids (were necessary illustrations provided and used in a manner relevant to the contents?)

4. Was the instructor well prepared?

5. Was the instructor effective in communicating concepts?

6. Accessibility of instructor (time for question, discussion)

Objective/Goals

1. Were learning clearly stated prior to the beginning of the program?

2. Degree to which your objective were met.

Content

1. Quality of class handouts and written materials.

2. Adequacy of time for covering each objective.

3. Degree of difficulty of the material (were you challenged)

4. Physical environment (was it conductive to learning)

5. Degree to which you feel the program will improve you.

6. How highly would you recommend this program to your peers?

How will you use what you learned from this program in your life?

Additional Comments:

Suggestions for Program improvement:

    (Please turn this in the facilitator at the end of the workshop)

Thank you Letter to the Speaker (after the event)

Date

Dear

Sincerely,

Recipe

Boiled Turkey Hindquarters (skin removed)
Eggs
Celery
Diced Real Onion
Pickled Relish
Mayonnaise, Mustard
Salt, Pepper, Seasoning Salt, Garlic Salt
Romaine Lettuce

Depending on the number of participants, 1 to 100, for every one turkey, two eggs, one or two stalks of celery, one small onion.

Mix all ingredients together, and make sure that the turkey ingredients is like making tuna, but turkey takes more mayonnaise and season to taste. Chill overnight.

Next morning, taste with a prayer from Jesus that it is delicious or add more seasonings and mayonnaise/mustard (not too much mustard).

One heartful scoop of turkey salad per leaf of romaine lettuce. Sprinkle paprika on top for the coloring.

Lovingly submitted by Sheila Guy-Snowden

NOTES

NOTES

NOTES

NOTES

About the Authors

NAOMI E. PEETE

A native of Baltimore, Maryland and the daughter of Elder Eddie and Ruth Peete, Naomi accepted Jesus Christ at an early age. Her highest aspiration is to teach and preach the gospel to all nations, as an ordained minister. She is the founder of On the Brink of Blessings Ministry, which has the main goals to educate, empower, equip and encourage men and women.

THERESA M. TAYLOR

Theresa is a native of Seattle, Washington. She proclaims Jesus Christ as her Lord and Savior. She is the wife of Larry Taylor, a Godly man and loving husband, for over thirty years. For twelve years, they lived in nine different states. Along the way, they raised two sons, Ethan and Jesse, who also know the Lord as their personal Savior.

Theresa has been working toward the purpose God created especially for her: an author who writes fiction which will help nurture those who are in need of emotional and spiritual encouragement and direction.

Bibliography

© 1997 Stephanie Nixon, Campus Involvement Center, University of Minnesota

© 1998 by the Regents of the University of Minnesota
The University of Minnesota is an equal opportunity educator and employer.
Last modified on July 27, 1998 by ocelx002@tc.umn.edu

Your Workday, Barbara Hemphill & Pamela Quinn Eibbard, Simpler Life, Reader's Digest, 1998, The Reader's Digest Assn., Inc. and Welden Owen Inc.

How to Make a Fortune from Public Speaking, Dr. Robert Anthony, Berkley, 1987

Living Your Christian Values, Ralph W. Neighbour, Jr., Convention Press, 1995

0-595-26792-0

www.ingramcontent.com/pod-product-compliance
Lightning Source LLC
Chambersburg PA
CBHW061247280526
45784CB00002B/667